W9-AOL-504

116332
Condoleezza Rice

Erinn Banting
AR B.L.: 5.5
Points: 0.5

REMARKABLE PEOPLE

Condoleezza Rice

by Erinn Banting

Published by Weigl Publishers Inc.
350 5th Avenue, Suite 3304, PMB 6G
New York, NY 10118-0069

Website: www.weigl.com
Copyright ©2008 WEIGL PUBLISHERS INC.

All of the Internet URLs given in the book were valid at the time of publication.
However, due to the dynamic nature of the Internet, some addresses may have
changed, or sites may have ceased to exist since publication. While the author and
publisher regret any inconvenience this may cause readers, no responsibility for any
such changes can be accepted by either the author or the publisher.

Library of Congress Cataloging-in-Publication Data

Banting, Erinn.
  Condoleezza Rice / Erinn Banting.
      p. cm. -- (Remarkable people)
  Includes index.
   ISBN 978-1-59036-639-4 (hard cover : alk. paper)--ISBN 978-1-59036-640-0 (soft
cover : alk. paper)
 1. Rice, Condoleezza, 1954--Juvenile literature. 2. Stateswomen--United States--
Biography--Juvenile literature. 3. Women cabinet officers--United States--Biography-
-Juvenile literature. 4. Cabinet officers--United States--Biography--Juvenile
literature. 5. National Security Council (U.S.)--Biography--Juvenile literature. 6.
African American women--Biography--Juvenile literature. 7. African Americans--
Biography--Juvenile literature. I. Title.
  E840.8.R48B36 2007
  327.730092--dc22
  [B]

                                   2006036966

Printed in the United States of America
1 2 3 4 5 6 7 8 9 0 11 10 09 08 07

Editor: Leia Tait
Design: Terry Paulhus

Cover: As U.S. secretary of state, Condoleezza Rice is one of the most powerful
women in the world.

Photograph Credits
Alabama Department of Archives and History, Montgomery, Alabama: page 7 top
left; Stanford News Service: page 17; University of Denver Special Collections &
Archives: pages 8, 14.

Every reasonable effort has been made to trace ownership and to obtain
permission to reprint copyright material. The publishers would be pleased to
have any errors or omissions brought to their attention so that they may be
corrected in subsequent printings.

Contents

Who Is Condoleezza Rice?

Condoleezza Rice has a successful career in education and politics. As a teacher, she has touched the lives of thousands of students. As a political figure, she influences world events. Condoleezza is the first African-American woman to hold the position of United States secretary of state. She is only the second woman in history to hold this position. As secretary of state, Condoleezza advises the president on events around the world. She helps shape the relationship her country has with the rest of the world. Condoleezza is passionate about learning and strives to make the world a better place.

> *"With education and hard work, it really does not matter where you come from—it matters where you are going."*

Growing Up

Condoleezza Rice was born on November 14, 1954. Her mother, Angelena, was a music teacher at a local high school. Condoleezza's father was Reverend John Wesley Rice, Jr. He worked as a guidance counselor at the same school where Condoleezza's mother taught. He was also a minister in the Presbyterian Church.

Condoleezza grew up in Birmingham, Alabama. During her childhood, Birmingham was a difficult place for African Americans to live. She and her family faced **discrimination**. Alabama had laws that supported **segregation**. These laws did not allow African Americans to have the same rights as others. African Americans could not attend certain schools and churches, or visit some public places, such as parks and restaurants. Condoleezza's father spoke out against segregation. He supported the Civil Rights Movement, a group that demanded **equality** for African Americans. They opposed people who believed in segregation. Confrontations between the groups often turned violent. To protect Condoleezza, her parents kept her close to home.

In 1963, Alabama Governor George C. Wallace blocked the door into the University of Alabama when African Americans attempted to sign up for classes.

Get to Know Alabama

COAT OF ARMS

FLAG

FLOWER
Camellia

Alabama became the 22nd state on December 14, 1819.

Alabama is located in the deep south, which is sometimes called Dixie. Alabama is known as "The Heart of Dixie."

Southern Alabama borders a body of water called the Gulf of Mexico.

Birmingham is the largest city in Alabama. Montgomery is the state capital.

The black bear is one of Alabama's official symbols.

Think about it!

Many people from Condoleezza's home state of Alabama had an important influence on U.S. history and the rights of African Americans. Research the Civil Rights Movement to learn more about the people who changed the lives of millions of African Americans. What influence do you think growing up in Alabama had on Condoleezza's future career?

Practice Makes Perfect

From an early age, Condoleezza loved to learn. She loved reading and music. Condoleezza had learned to read before she started school. When she was three, Condoleezza's mother taught her to play the piano. Condoleezza spent most of her childhood in Birmingham playing music and following her passion for learning. She studied French, music, art, and ballet.

In 1960, Condoleezza started school. Her abilities were so advanced that she skipped first grade. When she was in her early teens, Condoleezza's family moved to Denver, Colorado. There, she continued to pursue her love of learning. Condoleezza enrolled in St. Mary's Academy. It was the first non-segregated school she attended.

When she was a child, Condoleezza's parents gave her the nickname "Condi." Her close friends call her this today.

Condoleezza continued to do well in school. She skipped the seventh grade and qualified for university when she was only 15. Condoleezza did not want to attend university without her friends. She stayed in high school and took university classes part-time.

At first, Condoleezza struggled to find a subject she was excited about studying. One day, she attended a class by Dr. Josef Korbel. He taught **political science** at the Denver Graduate School of International Studies. During the class, Condoleezza became very interested in the things Dr. Korbel was saying. She decided to begin studying political science. Condoleezza realized that she could make a difference in the world if she followed her passion for education and politics.

Condoleezza still enjoys playing the piano. On April 22, 2002, she performed with well-known musician Yo-Yo Ma at a national arts awards ceremony.

Key Events

Condoleezza completed her **doctorate** in international studies in 1981. She then began teaching at Stanford University. While there, Condoleezza became an expert on the **Soviet Union**. U.S. political leaders began seeking her advice. In 1989, President George Bush made Condoleezza a member of the National Security Council. She was in charge of Soviet and East European affairs. The president was so impressed with Condoleezza's abilities that he asked her to be his special assistant on national security affairs.

During the 1990s, Condoleezza served as a political advisor while teaching at Stanford. She met the former president's son, George W. Bush. In 2000, George W. Bush ran for president. Condoleezza served as one of his advisors. Following his election, President George W. Bush made Condoleezza national security advisor. In 2005, he appointed her the 66th United States secretary of state.

■ Condoleezza was the first African-American woman to be made U.S. secretary of state.

Thoughts from Condoleezza

Condoleezza's love of learning about the world led her to a career in politics. Here are some of the things she has said about her life and career.

Condoleezza is a role model for many young people.

"I think you just go about your life, and if you're somehow inspiring to others, that's a good thing. Role models come in all shapes and sizes."

Condoleezza decides to study political science.

"It was like falling in love. I just suddenly knew that's what I wanted to do."

Condoleezza enjoys watching sports on television.

"Sports is a big element in my life. Football, hockey, basketball, sumo wrestling—anything with a score. I love the competition."

Condoleezza has big goals.

"My friends and I were raised to believe that we could do or become anything—that the only limits to our aspirations came from within."

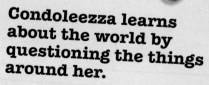

Condoleezza learns about the world by questioning the things around her.

"I tell my students, 'If you find yourself in the company of people who agree with you, you're in the wrong company.'"

Condoleezza becomes an advisor about the Soviet Union.

"It was great. I gained so much respect for military officers and what they do, and I think I really got an experience that few **civilians** have."

What Is a Secretary of State?

The secretary of state is the head of the U.S. Department of State. This department is part of the **executive branch** of government. It is in charge of **foreign affairs**. The State Department gathers, summarizes, and explains information about other countries. The president uses this information to decide how the United States will act in world affairs. The department then carries out the president's decisions.

Secretary of state is one of the highest offices in the U.S. government. As head of the Department of State, the secretary is the president's chief adviser on foreign affairs. He or she helps the president make decisions about the relationships the United States has with other countries. The secretary represents the president in dealings with foreign governments. The secretary of state is an important link between the United States and the rest of the world.

As secretary of state, Condoleezza often speaks to the United Nations (UN). This is an important organization made up of many of the world's countries.

Secretaries of State 101

Thomas Jefferson (1743–1826)

Term: 1790–1793

Achievements: Thomas Jefferson was the first U.S. secretary of state. He was appointed by President George Washington. Jefferson was a leading politician. He had spent five years in Paris as a foreign affairs minister. As the first secretary of state, Jefferson helped determine the United States' place in world affairs. He kept the country **neutral** during a war between Great Britain and France. Jefferson later became the third president of the United States.

Henry Kissinger (1923–)

Term: 1973–1977

Achievements: Henry Kissinger was the 56th U.S. secretary of state. He held the post under two presidents, Richard M. Nixon and Gerald R. Ford. Kissinger improved U.S. relations with many countries, including the Soviet Union, China, and Egypt. He helped remove the United States from the **Vietnam War**. In 1973, Kissinger brought about a peace agreement between North and South Vietnam. That year, he won the Nobel Peace Prize. This prize is given to people who have made a difference through their work towards peace and human rights.

Madeleine Albright (1937–)

Term: 1997–2001

Achievements: Madeleine Albright became the 64th U.S. secretary of state in 1997. She was the first woman to hold the position. Before becoming secretary, Albright served as the U.S. **ambassador** to the United Nations. As secretary of state, Albright strengthened U.S. relationships with many countries. She also promoted democracy and basic rights for people around the world.

Colin Powell (1937–)

Term: 2001–2005

Achievements: Colin Powell became the 65th U.S. secretary of state in 2001. He was the first African American to hold the position. Prior to becoming secretary, Powell served for many years in the U.S. army. He was an advisor to President Ronald Reagan between 1987 and 1989. Powell has received many awards, including two Presidential Medals of Freedom, the Congressional Gold Medal, and the Secretary of State Distinguished Service Medal.

The Great Seal

The U.S. secretary of state guards the Great Seal. This is a stamp that applies the U.S. coat of arms to official documents, such as **treaties** or letters to foreign leaders. The Great Seal is locked in a glass case inside the State Department. Members of the department must have the secretary of state's permission to stamp a document with the Great Seal.

Influences

As a university student, Condoleezza admired Dr. Josef Korbel. He was her teacher and her **mentor**. Korbel encouraged Condoleezza to study political science. He specifically urged her to study the Soviet Union. She took his advice. Studying the Soviet Union and its politics greatly helped Condoleezza in her political career.

The people who influenced Condoleezza the most were her family. They taught Condoleezza that she could achieve anything if she worked hard. Condoleezza's grandfather, John Wesley Rice, especially inspired her. John was descended from slaves. As a young man, he made very little money farming in Alabama. When John learned that Stillman College in Alabama accepted African-American students, he decided to attend the school. He saved money to pay for entrance. At the college, John studied to became a minister. He worked hard to finish his studies. Later, he started the Westminster Presbyterian Church in Birmingham.

Dr. Josef Korbel was Madeleine Albright's father. Condoleezza credits Korbel with helping her learn about political science.

Condoleezza's father felt deeply about the rights of African Americans. He taught Condoleezza to be proud of who she is. He also taught her to value education. Condoleezza's parents set an example by attending university. They believed in themselves. This gave Condoleezza the confidence she needed to hold one of the most important political offices in the world.

Martin Luther King, Jr. inspired Condoleezza's father in the 1960s. He continues to inspire Condoleezza today.

MARTIN LUTHER KING JR.

Many important events occurred in Birmingham during the Civil Rights Movement. In the early 1960s, Martin Luther King, Jr. led the African-American struggle for equality. He often made speeches and organized events in Birmingham. King inspired many people to speak out against discrimination and segregation. In 1968, he was **assassinated** because of these efforts. After his death, King became a symbol of courage, leadership, and equality for many people.

Overcoming Obstacles

As an African American, Condoleezza has faced **racism**. When she was a child, African Americans had to fight for equality. They often put their lives in danger to do so because some people opposed giving African Americans equal rights. When Condoleezza was eight years old, a man bombed the 16th Street Baptist church near her home. The church was attended by African Americans. One of Condoleezza's friends, Denise McNair, died in the bombing. Condoleezza's parents taught her not to be afraid. She never let others stop her from following her goals.

◼ On February 20, 2006, the 16th Street Baptist Church became a National Historic Landmark.

While some children her age did not finish high school, Condoleezza excelled at her studies. She completed each part of her education, from grade school to her doctorate, ahead of her classmates. Condoleezza's courage and intellect allowed her to overcome many obstacles. Few women have reached the same level of success in U.S. politics. Condoleezza is the first African-American woman to become secretary of state, the first to join the National Security Council, and the first to be appointed **provost** of Stanford University.

Condoleezza was Stanford's youngest and first female provost. In that position, she advised the head of the school. She helped shape what students learned.

Achievements and Successes

Condoleezza has achieved many things during her successful career. She has worked as an influential teacher and advisor to the U.S. government. As a political advisor, Condoleezza has influenced some of the world's most important events. She has received many awards recognizing her accomplishments. Universities throughout the United States have awarded Condoleezza with many honorary degrees. These degrees are given as tokens of honor or excellence. They recognize Condoleezza's hard work on behalf of the U.S. government. They also reward the gains she has made for women in U.S. politics.

On May 7, 2004, Condoleezza received an honorary degree from Michigan State University.

Condoleezza has had great success as a teacher. She has helped thousands of students learn about political science. She has won many teaching awards as a result. These include the Walter J. Gores Award for Excellence in Teaching and the Stanford University School of Humanities and Sciences Dean's Award for Distinguished Teaching.

Condoleezza's love of education has made her want to help students in other ways. In 1993, she helped found an after-school program for middle school students called the Center for a New Generation (CNG). The CNG provides students with opportunities to improve their education.

CENTER FOR A NEW GENERATION

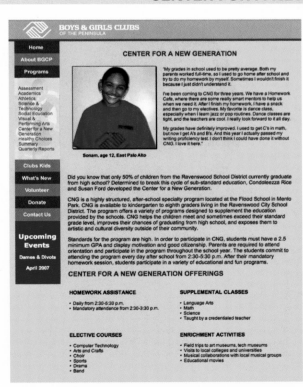

The Center for a New Generation (CNG) was started by Condoleezza Rice and Susan Ford Dorsey in 1993. CNG operates in the Ravenswood City School District in California. The program aims to improve students' chances of graduating from high school and attending college. CNG offers homework assistance, tutoring, art classes, and educational field trips. Nearly 100 percent of students who attend CNG graduate from high school and attend college. To learn more about CNG, visit their website at **www.bgcp.org/ cng_programs.php**.

Write a Biography

A person's life story can be the subject of a book. This kind of book is called a biography. Biographies describe the lives of remarkable people, such as those who have achieved great success or have done important things to help others. These people may be alive today or they may have lived many years ago. Reading a biography can help you learn more about a remarkable person.

At school, you might be asked to write a biography. First, decide who you want to write about. You can choose a political figure, such as Condoleezza Rice, or any other person you find interesting. Then, find out if your library has any books about this person. Learn as much as you can about him or her. Write down the key events in this person's life. What was this person's childhood like? What has he or she accomplished? What are his or her goals? What makes this person special or unusual?

A concept web is a useful research tool. Read the questions in the following concept web. Answer the questions in your notebook. Your answers will help you write your biography review.

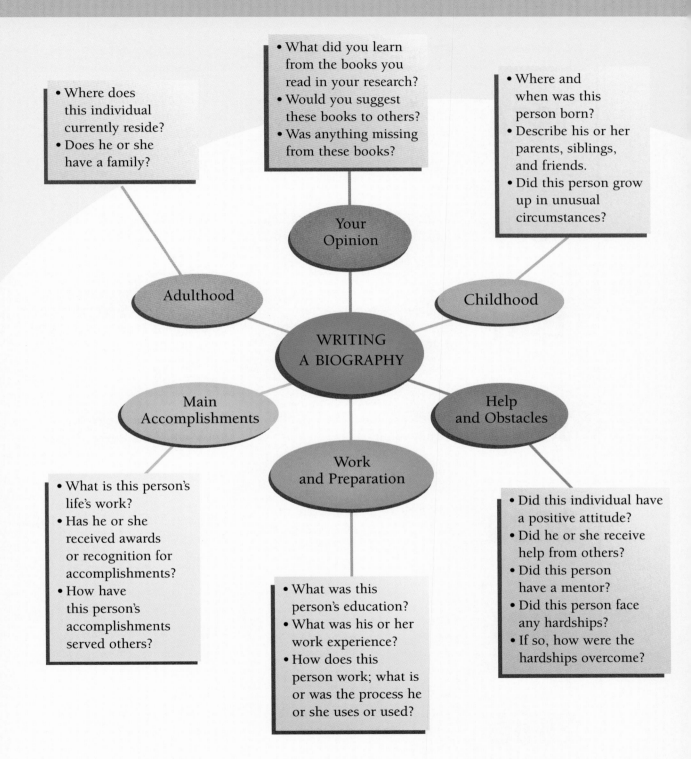

- What did you learn from the books you read in your research?
- Would you suggest these books to others?
- Was anything missing from these books?

- Where does this individual currently reside?
- Does he or she have a family?

- Where and when was this person born?
- Describe his or her parents, siblings, and friends.
- Did this person grow up in unusual circumstances?

Your Opinion

Adulthood

Childhood

WRITING A BIOGRAPHY

Main Accomplishments

Help and Obstacles

Work and Preparation

- What is this person's life's work?
- Has he or she received awards or recognition for accomplishments?
- How have this person's accomplishments served others?

- What was this person's education?
- What was his or her work experience?
- How does this person work; what is or was the process he or she uses or used?

- Did this individual have a positive attitude?
- Did he or she receive help from others?
- Did this person have a mentor?
- Did this person face any hardships?
- If so, how were the hardships overcome?

Timeline

YEAR	CONDOLEEZZA RICE	WORLD EVENTS
1954	Condoleezza is born on November 14 in Birmingham, Alabama.	The Geneva Conference begins in Switzerland. At the conference, world leaders discuss restoring peace in Asia.
1974	At age 19, Condoleezza graduates from the University of Denver.	President Richard M. Nixon resigns on August 8.
1981	Condoleezza receives her doctorate from the University of Denver.	In November, representatives from the United States and the Soviet Union meet to discuss the reduction of nuclear weapons in Europe.
1989	Condoleezza joins the National Security Council.	George Bush becomes the 41st president of the United States.
2000	Condoleezza helps George W. Bush win the presidential election, which takes place on November 7.	In March, Vladimir Putin is elected president of Russia.
2001	Condoleezza becomes national security advisor on January 22.	Terrorists attack the World Trade Center in New York City on September 11.
2005	Condoleezza is sworn in as the 66th U.S. secretary of state on January 28.	The first democratic elections in Iraq since 1958 take place on January 30.

Further Research

How can I find out more about Condoleezza Rice?

Most libraries have computers that connect to a database for searching for information. If you input a key word, you will be provided with a list of books in the library that contain information on that topic. Non-fiction books are arranged numerically, using their call number. Fiction books are organized alphabetically by the author's last name.

Websites

To learn more about Condoleezza Rice, visit
www.whitehouse.gov/nsc/ricebio.html

To learn more about the Department of State, visit
http://future.state.gov/

Words to Know

ambassador: a government official who represents his or her country in other parts of the world

assassinated: murdered for political reasons

civilians: people not in the armed forces

discrimination: unfair treatment of a person or group based on race, culture, or religion

doctorate: the highest degree a person can receive from university

equality: when all persons or things are treated the same

executive branch: the part of the U.S. government that ensures people follow the laws; this branch includes the president

foreign affairs: interactions with other nations

mentor: a wise and trusted teacher

neutral: not taking a side in a conflict

political science: the study of governments and their workings

provost: someone who oversees the management of a university

racism: treating people poorly because of their race

segregation: the practice of setting one racial group apart from another

Soviet Union: a group of countries, including Russia, that were once united

treaties: agreements between different countries

Vietnam War: a war in southeastern Asia that lasted from 1957 to 1975

Index